P9-DEB-630

Social Studies Alive!™

My Community

Teachers' Curriculum Institute

Bert Bower Jim Lobdell

Managing Editor: Laura M. Alavosus
Project Editor: Wendy Frey
Production Editor: Mali Apple
Editorial Assistant: Anna Embree
Art Director: Tim Stephenson
Production Coordinator: Lynn Sanchez
Senior Graphic Designer: Christy Uyeno
Graphic Designers: Katy Haun, Victoria Philp,
Paul Rebello
Photographer: Tim Stephenson
Photo Acquisitions: Anna Embree
Audio and Photography Director: Katy Haun
Operations Manager: Ellen Mapstone

This book is published by Teachers' Curriculum Institute.

Teachers' Curriculum Institute
PO Box 50996
1170 East Meadow Drive
Palo Alto, CA 94303

Customer Service: 800-497-6138
www.socialstudiesalive.net

ISBN 1-58371-276-3
2 3 4 5 6 7 8 9 10 07 06 05 04 03

Program Directors

Bert Bower

Jim Lobdell

Program Author

Vicki LaBoskey, Professor of Education,
Mills College, Oakland, California
Ph.D., Curriculum and Teacher Education,
Stanford University, Stanford, California

Student Edition/Big Book Authors

Laura M. Alavosus

Wendy Frey

Senior Curriculum Developer

Joyce Bartky

Reading Specialist

Barbara Schubert, Reading Specialist,
Saint Mary's College, Moraga, California
Ph.D., Education: International Studies,
University of Santa Barbara, Santa Barbara,
California

Teacher Consultants

Jill Bartky, Elementary Teacher,
Sharp Park Elementary School, Pacifica,
California

Debra Elsen, Elementary Teacher,
Manchester Elementary, Manchester, Maryland

Beth Yankee, Elementary Teacher,
The Woodward School for Technology and
Research, Kalamazoo, Michigan

Internet and Literature Consultant

Debra Elsen, Elementary Teacher,
Manchester Elementary, Manchester, Maryland

Music Specialist

Beth Yankee, Elementary Teacher,
The Woodward School for Technology and
Research, Kalamazoo, Michigan

Geography Specialist

David Knipfer
Mapping Specialists, Ltd.
Madison, Wisconsin

Contents

12

CITY COUNCIL

TRAILER PARK
FIRE DEPARTMENT
CITY HALL
PETE'S FOODS
THEATER
CHO'S DINER
JULIA'S

What Is a Community?

In this chapter, you will learn that a **community** is a place where people live, work, and play. A community is also a place where people solve problems together.

A Place to Live

A community is a place where people live. Some people live in houses. Some people live in **apartments**. Some people live in mobile homes. Does everyone have a home to live in?

A Place to Work

A community is a place where people work. Some people work in offices. Some people work in factories. Others work in stores and **restaurants**. Some people work indoors. Some people work outdoors. Where do people work in your community?

A Place to Play

A community is a place where people play. People like to have fun. Many people have fun at playgrounds. Some people like to go to movies. Others have fun at **museums**. Where do you have fun in your community?

A Place to Solve Problems

A community is a place where people solve problems together. Sometimes people go to city hall to solve problems together. Sometimes they meet at a school. Some people go to community centers to solve problems together. Where do people solve problems in your community?

Wrap-Up

A community is a place where people live, work, and play. A community is also a place where people solve problems together.

How Are Communities Different?

All communities are not the same. In this chapter, you will learn about three kinds of communities. They are called **urban, rural,** and **suburban**.

Cities Are Urban Communities

Cities have lots of buildings and people. People often walk from place to place in a city. Sometimes they take a bus or a taxi. Many people ride trains from one part of a city to another. Some people drive cars.

People live in apartments in cities. There might be 50 or more homes in an apartment building. Where do you live?

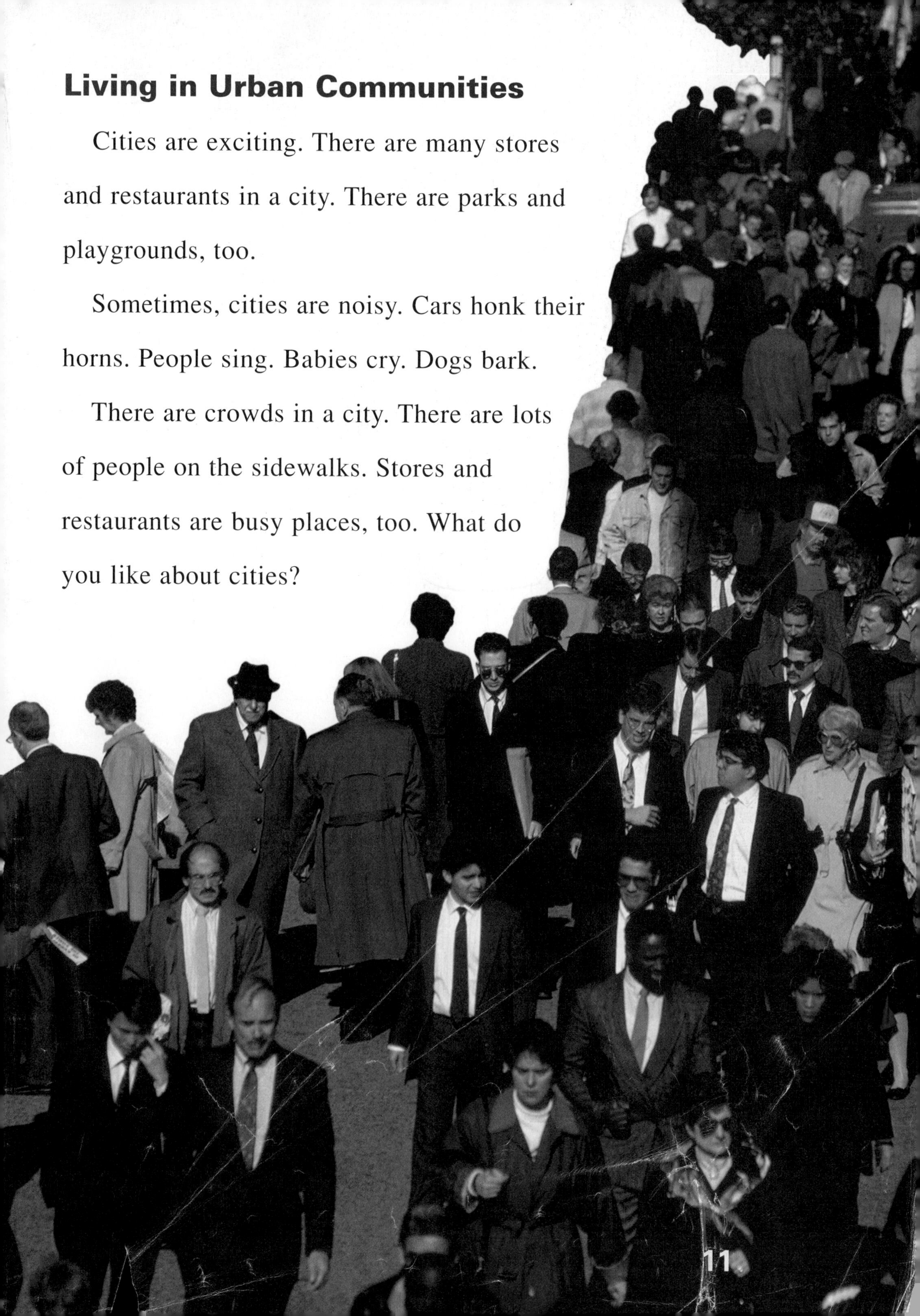

Living in Urban Communities

Cities are exciting. There are many stores and restaurants in a city. There are parks and playgrounds, too.

Sometimes, cities are noisy. Cars honk their horns. People sing. Babies cry. Dogs bark.

There are crowds in a city. There are lots of people on the sidewalks. Stores and restaurants are busy places, too. What do you like about cities?

Small Towns Are Rural Communities

Small towns are in the countryside. They are far from cities.

Small towns have fewer people than cities. Everybody knows their neighbors in a small town.

Small towns might have just one store. There may be a post office, a bank, and a school. Do you live in a small town?

Living in Rural Communities

Many people live and work on farms in rural communities. They drive to the store and the post office. Kids ride a bus to school.

There are different ways to have fun in a small town. In a city, you might visit a big aquarium. In a small town, you might go fishing. What would you do in a small town?

Suburbs Are Suburban Communities

Suburban communities are called **suburbs**. Suburbs are smaller than cities. They are bigger than small towns.

There are neighborhoods full of homes in suburbs. There are schools, fire stations, police stations, and hospitals. There are stores and gas stations. There are parks and other places to play. Do you live in a suburb?

Living in Suburban Communities

Many families live in suburbs. Some people live in houses. Some people live in apartments. Lots of homes have yards.

Most people drive cars in a suburb. People drive to work. They drive to shopping malls. There are lots of parking lots in suburbs. What else might you see in a suburb?

Wrap-Up

There are different kinds of communities. People live in urban communities. People also live in rural and suburban communities.

JOE'S DELI
ICE CREAM
CITY PARK
KEY
Merry-go-round
Picnic area
Play-ground
Rest rooms
Sand area
Swan boats
NORTH
YOU ARE HERE

What Does a Map Show?

Let's learn about maps. A map is a drawing of a place or a community. It shows what a place looks like from above. A map has **symbols**. It also has a **key,** a **grid,** and a **compass rose**. You will learn to use these things to read a map.

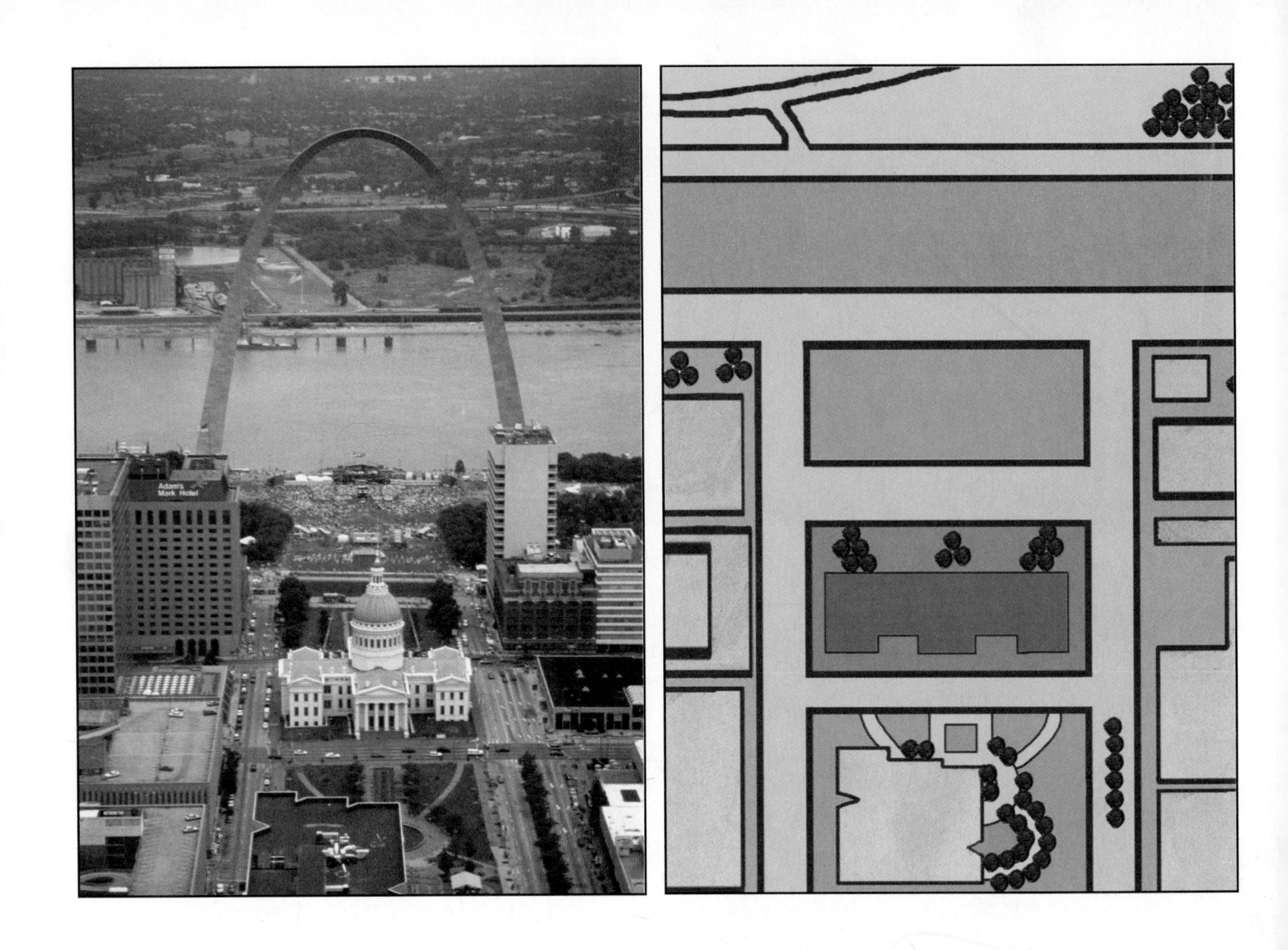

A Map Shows a Place

A map is a drawing of a place. It shows what the place looks like from above. The map is smaller than the place. It does not show everything in that place.

Look at the picture of the city above. Now look at the map of that city.

What buildings does the map show?

A Map Has a Key

Some keys open doors. Other keys are clues about new things. A map key gives clues about important things on the map.

The pictures on a map are called symbols. The map key tells us what these symbols mean.

How many symbols do you see on this map?

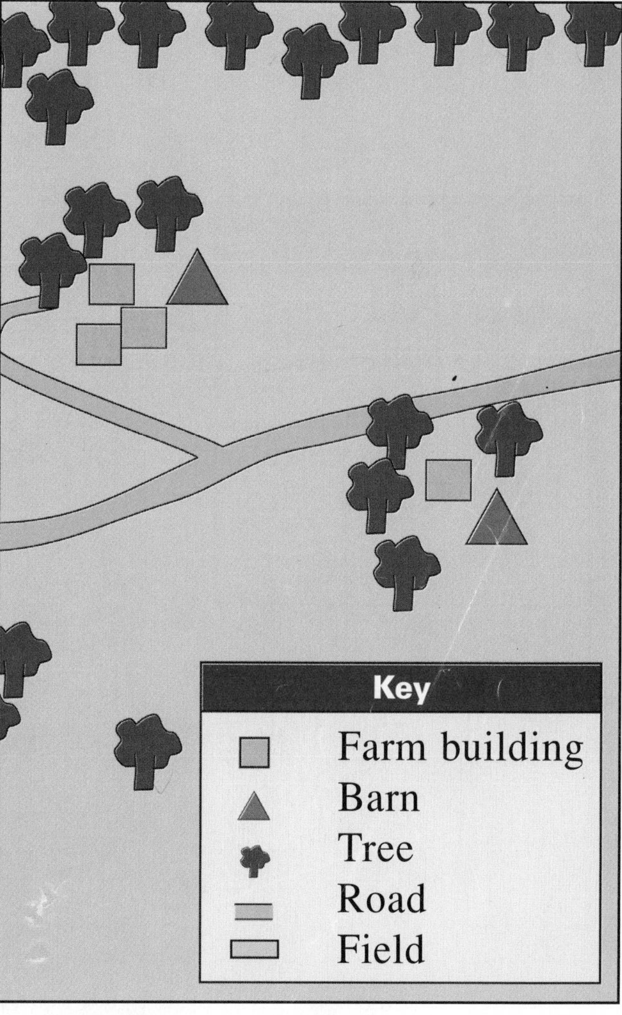

A Map Has a Grid

A map grid is a set of lines that cross each other. The lines make squares all over the map. Each row has a letter. Each column has a number.

The grid helps us find places on the map. We can follow a letter and a number to find squares on the grid.

Look at the grid on this map. What is in Square A2?

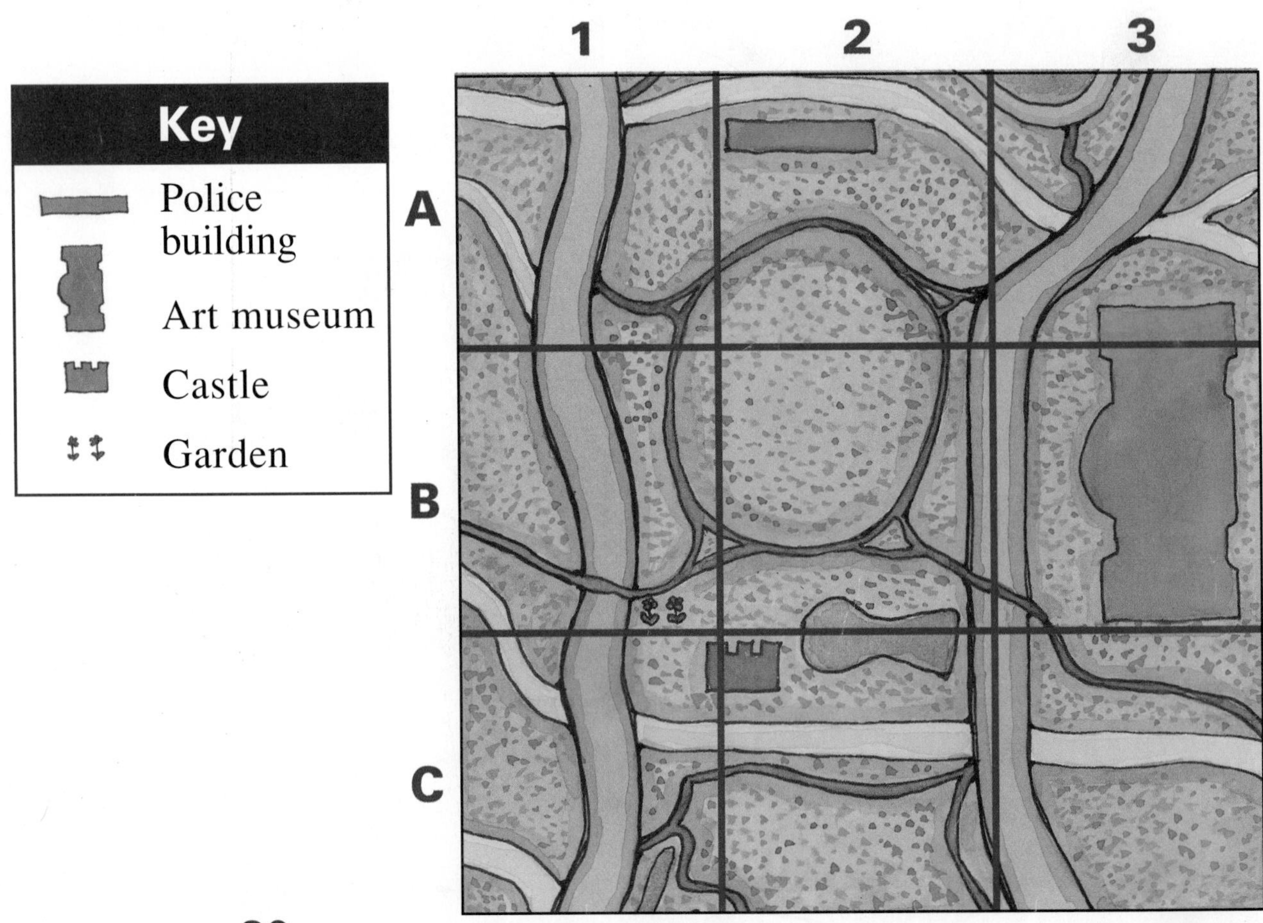

A Map Has a Compass Rose

A **compass** points to the directions north, south, east, and west. A compass rose is a drawing of a compass on a map. It shows the directions on a map.

Look at this map. What building is north of the hospital?

Wrap-Up

A map shows what places look like from above. A map has a key. A map has a grid. A map also has a compass rose.

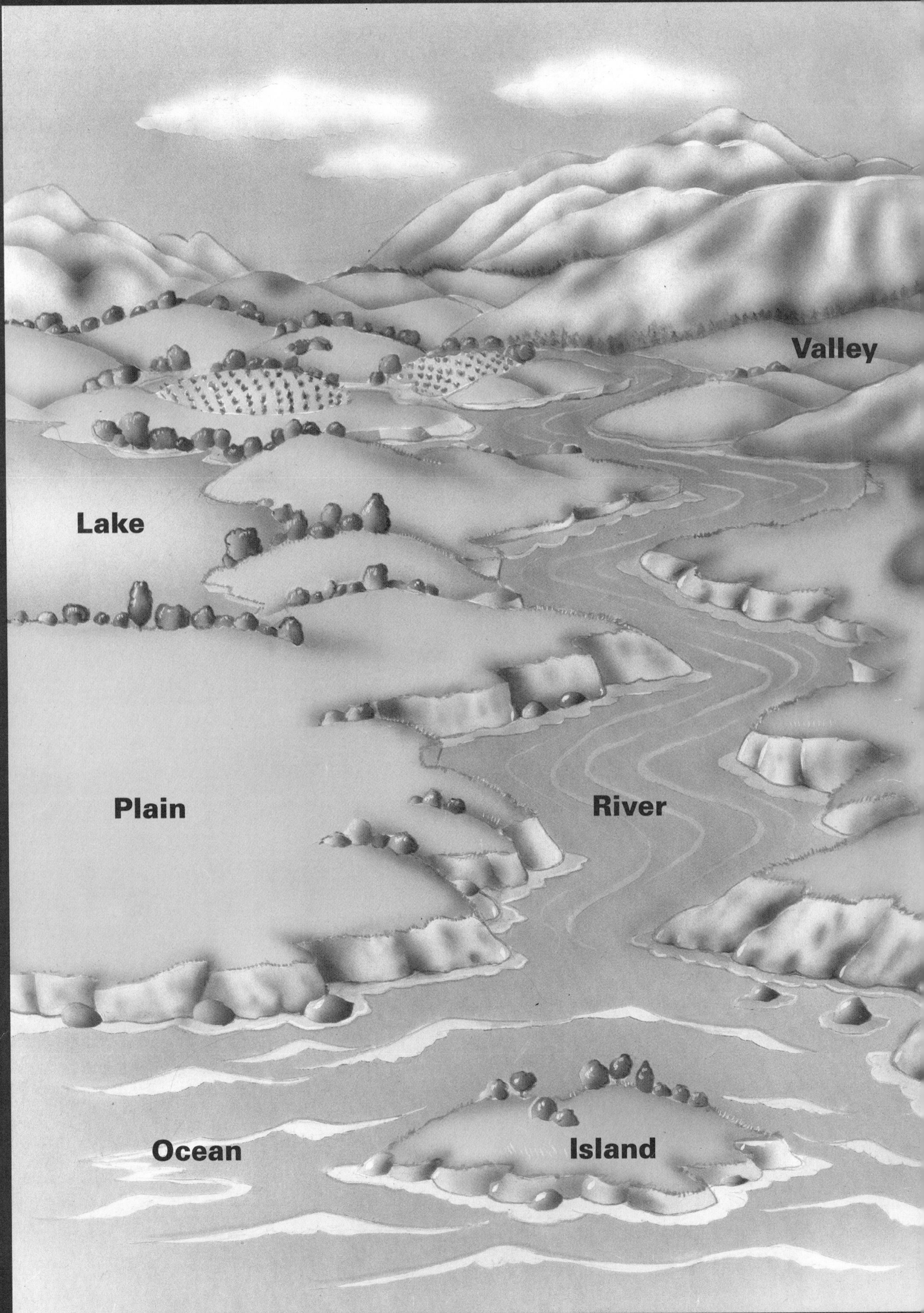

Valley

Lake

Plain

River

Ocean

Island

What Is Geography?

Communities are in many different places. Some are near water. Some are near mountains. The land and water around a community is called geography. Every community has its own **geography**.

In this chapter, you will learn about the geography in different communities. You will discover the features of geography on a map.

Mountains and Valleys

Mountains are the tallest kind of land on Earth. Mountains have many trees. It snows on mountains in the winter.

Valleys are low places between mountains. Most valleys have rivers. Snow melts off the mountains and fills the rivers.

There are communities on mountains. There are communities in valleys. Do you live near mountains and valleys?

Deserts and Plains

Deserts are places that get very little rain. Deserts are very hot in the summer. Deserts are not good places to grow crops. People in desert communities learn not to waste water.

Plains are large areas of flat land. Plains get more rain than deserts. Plains are good places to grow crops and raise animals. Are there farms in your community?

Rivers and Lakes

A **river** is a body of water that moves through land. People and goods can travel on rivers. Some rivers flow through communities. People swim and boat in rivers.

Lakes are bodies of water with land all around them. Lots of people like living near lakes. They can go fishing, swimming, and boating. Do you live near a river or lake?

Oceans and Islands

An **island** is land that has water all around it. There are islands in lakes and in **oceans**. Oceans are the largest bodies of water on Earth.

Some islands are small places. They don't have everything that people need. Things are sent to islands on ships and airplanes. Have you ever lived on an island?

Kinds of Maps

There are many kinds of maps. Some maps show streets. Some show states and countries. Others show crops or numbers of people in different areas. There are even maps that show the weather in different places. What might a map of your community show?

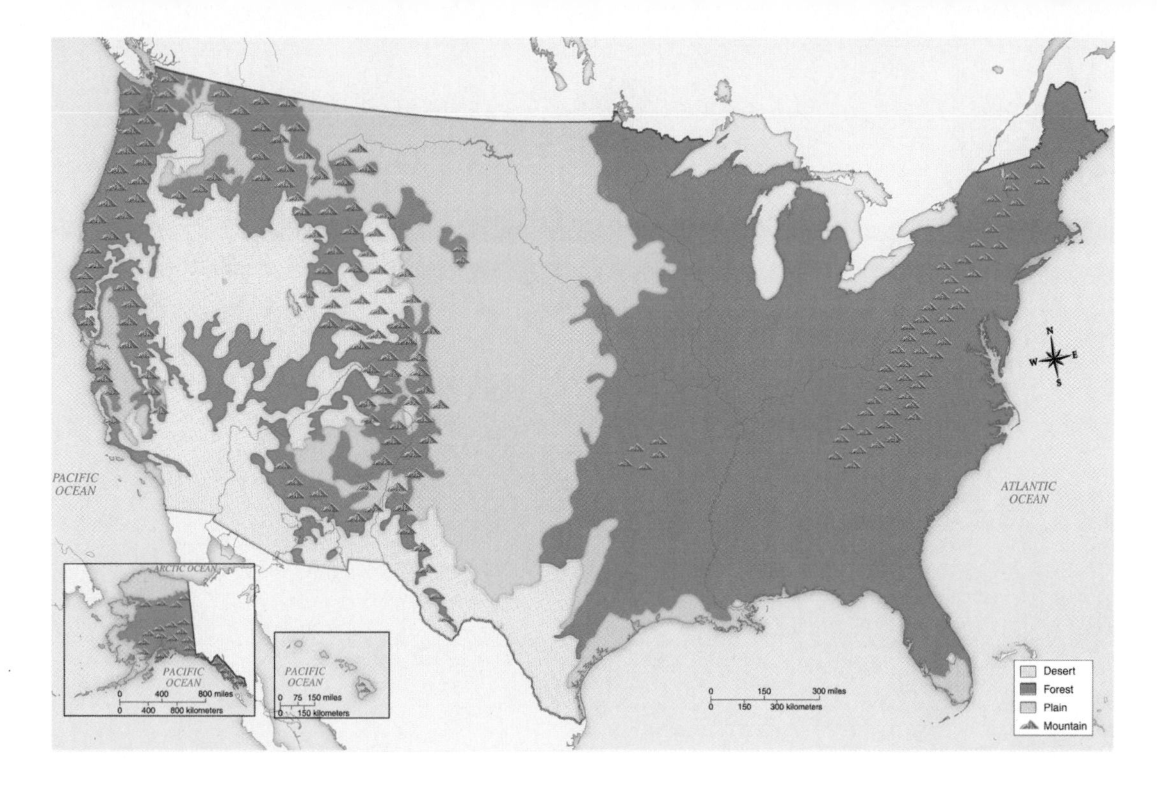

Physical Maps

Some maps show land and bodies of water. They are called physical maps. They use colors and symbols to show mountains, plains, and deserts. You can also find rivers, lakes, and oceans on this kind of map. What does this map show?

Wrap-Up

People live in communities near mountains, deserts, or plains. Other communities are by oceans, rivers, or lakes. Maps can show features of geography.

How Do People Use the Environment?

Our **environment** is all around us. Land, plants, and animals are all part of the environment.

In this chapter, you will learn how people use things in their environment. Then you will learn how **pollution** hurts our environment.

Nature Is Important to Us

Plants and animals are part of nature. So are trees and stones.

People use nature to make objects they want and need. They use plants and animals for food and clothing. They use trees and stones for houses.

Look all around you. What things are part of nature? What things are made by people?

We Live in Many Different Environments

Different environments have different land, weather, plants, and animals.

Some places have mountains. Some have deserts. Some have rivers or oceans.

Some places have hot weather. Some are cold. Some are wet, and some are dry.

Different places have different plants and animals.

Look around you. What is your environment like?

Using Nature for Food

We use plants and animals for food. Different foods come from different environments.

Fish live in oceans, lakes, and rivers. Cows live in places where there is grass. We raise pigs, sheep, goats, and chickens for food.

Farmers grow crops for food. Some crops, like wheat, grow best on the plains where the weather is hot and dry. Other plants need warm, rainy environments.

Look around you. What kind of food could you catch, gather, or grow in your environment?

Using Nature to Make Clothing

We use plants and animals to make clothing. Cotton comes from a plant. It grows only where the climate is warm. We get wool from sheep. Sheep need grass to eat.

Look around you. What clothing comes from the plants and animals in your environment?

Using Nature to Make Shelter

We use nature to make shelter. People use wood to make homes. Wood comes from trees in the forest. People use stones to build homes. Stones can be found in many different places. People also use the earth to make homes. In the desert, they mix straw and mud to make bricks.

Look around you. What could you use to make shelter in your environment?

Polluting Our Water

Sometimes people don't take care of the Earth's water.

They throw garbage in rivers, lakes, and streams. They let chemicals spill in the ocean. This is called water pollution.

Water pollution means people can't drink or swim in the water. Fish and other animals that live in the water may die.

What can you do to help keep our water clean and safe?

Spoiling Our Land

Sometimes people don't take care of the land.

They cut down too many trees. They dump trash on the land. They bury poisons in the earth. This is called land pollution.

We share the land with plants and animals. When we spoil the land, plants cannot grow in the earth. Animals may die, because they have no food to eat or places to live.

What can you do to help keep the land clean and beautiful?

Polluting Our Air

Sometimes people don't take care of the air.

Factories and cars fill the air with smoke. This is called air pollution.

When the air is dirty, it is hard for people to breathe. Animals can get sick, too.

What can you do to help keep the air clean?

Wrap-Up

Our environment is all around us. We use our environment for food, clothing, and shelter. People, plants, and animals all need clean water, clean land, and clean air.

CHAPTER 6

How Are Goods Made and Brought to Us?

Today, most people in the United States do not grow their own food or make their own clothes. Instead, they buy them.

In this chapter, you will learn how **goods** are grown on farms and made in factories. You will also read about the different kinds of **transportation** that bring goods to stores.

Farmers Grow Our Food

Farmers grow most of our food for us. Some farmers grow wheat. Some farmers grow corn. Some farmers grow tomatoes.

Some farms are small. Some farms are large, with lots of land for growing crops.

Some farms are near the ocean. Some farms are in the middle of the country.

What foods can you name that grow on farms?

People Make Other Goods in Factories

Most of our other goods, like toys and clothing, are made in factories.

Factories often have large machines and many workers. Each worker does one small part of the whole job. Together, they make one product.

What things can you name that come from factories?

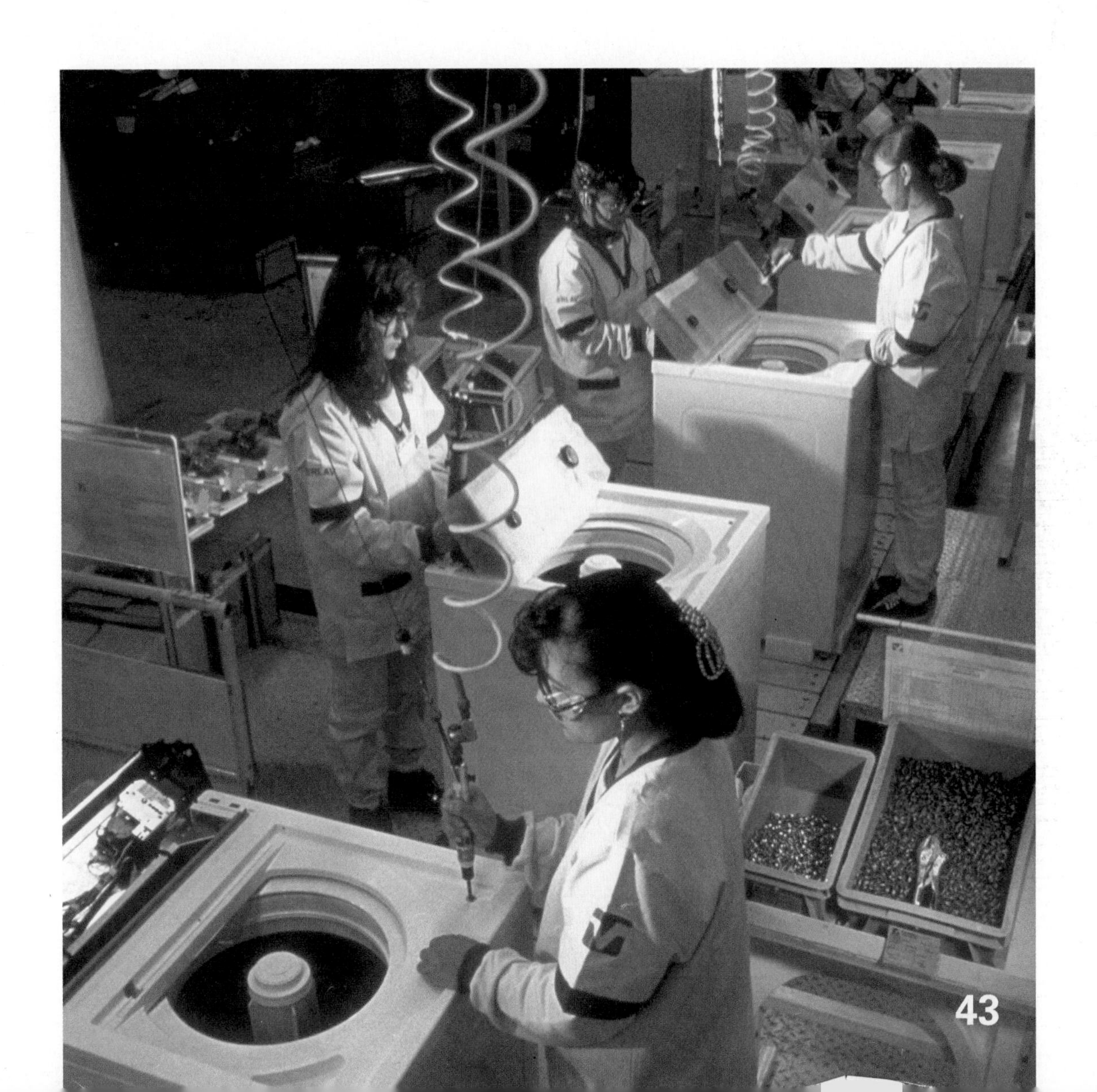

A Busy Shirt Factory

It takes many workers to make one shirt.

One worker cuts shirt pieces from cloth. Another sews the pieces together. A third worker sews on buttons and makes buttonholes. Other workers add pockets and labels.

Finally, one person makes sure that the shirt is perfect. Then it is ready to be ironed and wrapped.

How many workers do you think made the shirt you are wearing?

How Goods Are Brought to Stores

Goods are loaded onto trucks at the farm and at the factory. The trucks take the goods to warehouses. The goods stay at the warehouses until it is time for them to be brought to the stores.

People use many different kinds of transportation to bring goods to the stores. Some goods travel in planes. Some goods cross oceans in ships. Some goods travel by train. Some goods are driven in trucks.

How do you think the goods in your home were brought to the store?

From Around the World to Our Community

All over the world, people grow and make the goods we need and want.

Some goods come from India. Some goods come from Japan. We use transportation to move goods from one community to another.

What goods can you name that were made far away?

From the Store to You

We buy the goods we need and want in stores.

There are many kinds of stores. There are stores that sell food. There are stores that sell clothes. There are stores that sell toys.

How many different kinds of stores are in your community?

Wrap-Up

Many of our goods are made by teams of workers in factories. Each person on the team does one job. We use planes, ships, trains, and trucks to move goods around the world.

12

Who Provides Services in a Community?

Some people have jobs helping other people. Those jobs are called **service jobs**.

In this chapter, you will learn about the people who provide services in the community.

People Who Give Us Ideas

Some people give us ideas.

Authors share ideas by writing books, plays, and poems.

Television reporters brings us news and ideas from TV studios. They also go to places where the news is happening.

Architects have ideas about what a building will look like. They draw their ideas on a piece of paper called a blueprint.

Can you think of other jobs like these?

People Who Fix Things

Some people fix things.

Plumbers put water pipes into buildings. They also fix pipes when they break.

Electricians work with electricity. They put electric wires in buildings and repair things that use electricity.

Mechanics fix cars when they break down. They change tires that are flat or worn out. They put new parts in our cars.

Can you think of other jobs like these?

People Who Take Care of Us and Our Pets

Some people take care of people or pets.

Child-care workers take care of children when parents are working.

Doctors help people stay healthy. If we are sick, a doctor may give us medicine to help us get better.

Our pets have special doctors called veterinarians. They take care of sick or injured animals.

Can you think of other jobs like these?

People Who Entertain Us

Some people work to entertain others.

Musicians play musical instruments to make music. They may work alone, in a small group, or in a large band.

Actors are people who pretend to be someone or something else. They often wear makeup and costumes.

Athletes are people who are good at sports. There are many kinds of athletes. People enjoy watching athletes play football, basketball, baseball, and other games.

Wrap-Up

Some people have service jobs. They give us ideas. They fix things. They take care of people and animals. They entertain others.

RETURNS
NEW!
SCOOTERS
SOLD OUT!
NEW!
Balls

How Can I Be a Good Shopper?

People use money to buy the things they **need** and **want**.

In this chapter, you will learn how to make good decisions when you go shopping.

We Need Money to Buy Things

We all need money to buy goods and services. Most people earn money by making goods or doing a service.

Some people have a lot of money. They can buy the things they need and want easily.

Some people have little or no money. They cannot always buy what they need and want.

What do you buy with your money?

We Make Choices When We Shop

We go shopping to buy the things we need and want.

Shopping can be fun. But shopping isn't always easy.

There are a lot of choices to make when we go shopping. Should we buy a drink from a machine or from a store? Should we shop at a big store, or a smaller store close to home?

Where do you go shopping?

We Buy What We Need

There is a difference between what we need and what we want.

People need food. People need clothing. People need shelter. People sometimes want things they don't really need. You may want lots of toys. You may need a new pair of shoes.

We make a good choice when we buy the things we need first.

What things do you need? What things do you want?

We Are Wise Shoppers

How can you be a wise shopper? Here are some hints.

Look for the best things.

Look for the best price.

Keep your sales receipt. If something is wrong with what you buy, you may be able to return it to the store.

How are you a wise shopper?

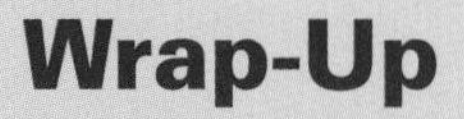

Wrap-Up

People use money to buy things. They go shopping for goods and services. Wise shoppers buy what they need first. Then they buy the things they want.

EVERGREEN
HOMES
FOR SALE
MiNi-MART
GAS
OPEN
SALE

How Do Communities Change?

Sometimes communities grow bigger. Sometimes communities get smaller.

In this chapter, you will look at how one city changed over time. You will see how people made their city a better place to live.

Communities Change over Time

Communities grow bigger when people move to them. Communities get smaller when people move away from them.

People move to a community for many reasons. Some people come for a new job. Some people want to live in a different home.

People move away from communities for many reasons, too. Some people change jobs. Some people want to live in a different town.

People Move to a Community

Look at this picture of a steel mill in Pittsburgh, Pennsylvania. Many people moved to Pittsburgh to work in this mill.

The new people needed many things. They needed homes. They needed stores. They needed schools for their children.

People built new buildings and other places. The community grew bigger.

People Move Away from a Community

One day, the steel mill closed. People moved away from Pittsburgh.

Some of the stores closed. Some of the buildings were left empty.

No one took care of the empty buildings. They started to fall apart.

People Work to Make Their Communities Better

Some people wanted to make Pittsburgh beautiful again. They fixed old buildings. They built new places. They wanted people to move back to their city.

Look around you. What changes do you see in your community?

Wrap-Up

Communities grow bigger as people move to them. Communities get smaller as people move away. Some people make their communities better. They fix old buildings. They build new places. They care about their communities.

How Did One Community Change?

You have learned that communities grow and change. This is how cities and towns create history. **History** is what has happened in the past.

In this chapter, you will read how one community changed. San Francisco grew from a small town into a large city.

San Francisco Was a Small Town

San Francisco is next to the Pacific Ocean. It has a harbor for ships. Long ago, many big sailing ships stopped in the harbor.

Many people on the ships decided to live in San Francisco. They built houses and stores.

The sailors on the ships needed supplies. So, people built stores for them. Others built hotels for people who just came to visit.

This is how the town of San Francisco started to grow.

Gold Is Found

In 1848, people found gold near San Francisco. The word spread quickly all over the world. Many people traveled to San Francisco to look for gold. They came from other parts of our country. They came from countries far away. They came in ships. They came on horses.

Now there were many more people in San Francisco. They all needed places to eat and sleep. They needed lots of other things, too.

San Francisco Grows Into a City

People who look for gold are called gold miners. Gold miners stopped in San Francisco on their way to find gold.

The miners needed food, clothing, and tents. They needed shovels and pans.

Soon there were new stores and shops in San Francisco. The miners kept coming. More people arrived to open more shops. They built more roads and houses, too.

Life in the City

Life in the city was not easy. There were many new people. Now people had to wait in line at the stores. The streets were muddy from all the horses.

There were not enough firefighters to keep the city safe. The new houses were built of wood. People used oil and gas lamps to see at night. These lamps caused fires easily.

But San Francisco still kept growing.

A Timeline of the San Francisco Earthquake in 1906

The earth shook.

The fires blazed.

Wednesday

Thursday

Friday

The San Francisco Earthquake

By 1906, San Francisco was a large city. Then a terrible **earthquake** happened. An earthquake makes the ground shake.

Many buildings fell down. Others caught fire and burnt to the ground. The fires spread all over the city. Many people lost their homes.

After the earthquake, people lived in tents in the city park. They were afraid to go near the rest of the buildings. They cooked their food outdoors.

After a while, people began to build their homes and shops again.

The wharves are saved.

Saturday

The city will rebuild.

Sunday

Timeline of the 1906 Earthquake

Timelines show when things happen. They can show things that happened over many years.

Look at this timeline. It tells the story of the San Francisco earthquake. This was a big event in the history of San Francisco. Even today, people think about it.

Wrap-Up

San Francisco was a small town. Then people found gold. The town grew into a city. An earthquake made many buildings fall down. People built the city back up again.

How Can One Person Make a Difference in a Community?

All communities have problems to solve. Cities have different problems than communities in the country. Sometimes one person thinks of an idea that will make a community better.

In this chapter, you will learn about four people from the past who helped their communities.

Jane Addams Gave Children a Place to Play

Jane Addams lived from 1860 to 1935. She lived in the city of Chicago, Illinois. She saw children playing in the streets of her city. She knew they were not safe.

Jane wanted to help. Soon she had an idea. She rented a building where children could play and be safe. She called it "Hull House." Jane also built Chicago's first playground.

Jane Addams saw a problem in her community and solved it.

Garrett August Morgan Made His Community Safer

Garrett Morgan lived from 1877 to 1963. He lived in Cleveland, Ohio. He was an inventor.

Garrett saw that the streets of his city were getting very crowded. Cars often crashed into each other where streets crossed. Drivers did not know when it was their turn to go.

Garrett invented the first traffic light. It had arms that moved up and down. The arms showed drivers when to stop and when to go.

Garrett's idea helped keep the people of Cleveland safe.

Susan LaFlesche Picotte Helped Sick People Get Better

Susan Picotte lived from 1865 to 1915. She was a Native American. Susan lived in a community in the state of Nebraska. People in her community got sick from time to time. But, there was no doctor to help them.

Susan grew up and went away to school. She studied hard and became a doctor.

Dr. Picotte rode a horse to visit her patients. Later, she started a hospital.

Susan helped her community by becoming a doctor and caring for people when they got sick.

Luis Valdez Helped Farmworkers Have Better Lives

Luis Valdez was born in 1940. He lived in a community of farmworkers. He knew they worked hard. He knew they didn't have nice homes.

Luis wrote plays about how hard their lives were. He took actors from farm to farm on trucks. They performed his plays in the fields.

Many farmworkers saw his plays. Luis helped people by teaching them that they could have better lives.

Wrap-Up

All communities have problems to solve. Sometimes one person thinks of an idea to make a community better.

CITY · COUNCIL
CITY · SEAL

How Do Leaders Help Their Communities?

Leaders are people who help make important decisions.

In this chapter, you will learn how communities choose leaders. You will also learn what community leaders do to help their communities.

People Vote for Leaders

In most communities, people choose leaders by voting for them.

People who want to be leaders tell the community their ideas. Then, adults in the community vote for the person they think will be a good leader.

Leaders have many important jobs to do. It can be fun to be a leader.

Leaders Help Make Laws

Community leaders help make laws for the community. A **law** is a rule.

Some laws help people stay safe. There are laws to tell people how fast they should drive. There are laws to tell people where they can ride their bicycles and skateboards.

Some laws help the community stay clean and beautiful. There are laws to stop people from throwing garbage on the ground. There are laws about where it is okay to walk a dog in the city.

Leaders Pay for Services

Community leaders decide how to spend the community's money.

Every community needs people to help keep it safe. This is the job of firefighters and police. Leaders decide how much money to spend on firefighters and police.

Every community needs people to work on its streets and sidewalks. Community leaders decide how much money to pay these workers.

Leaders Decide What to Build

Community leaders decide where to build new buildings and parks.

Leaders think about whether a new building is really needed. They also think about what buildings will look like.

These decisions help make sure everyone can enjoy the buildings and parks in a community.

Wrap-Up

People choose leaders to make important decisions. Leaders make laws for the community. They decide what services to pay for. They decide what buildings and parks to build in the community.

CHAPTER 13

What Does a Good Citizen Do?

Community leaders work hard to make their community a good place to live. Everyone has to help.

In this chapter, you will learn what you can do to be a good **citizen**.

Communities Need Good Citizens

People who live in communities are called citizens. Good citizens work to make their communities better.

Grown-up citizens vote for community leaders. They obey the laws. They help keep their communities clean and safe.

Children cannot vote. But they can be good citizens. They can obey the laws. They can help make their communities better.

Good Citizens Get Along with Others

Good citizens get to know people on the inside. Good citizens don't tease or call people names. They are kind to others.

Good citizens listen to what other people say. They solve problems by talking.

If a problem is serious, good citizens know how to ask for help.

Good Citizens Help Others

There are many ways to be a good citizen by helping others. Here are some ideas.

Good citizens collect food and clothes for people who need them. Visit a sick friend. Or call someone who is lonely.

Good citizens make decorations for a hospital. Visit someone in a nursing home. Or send a card to someone who is sad.

Good citizens carry packages for an older person. Help someone clean up a yard.

Or help a younger child make something.

What other ways can you think of to help people?

Good Citizens Help Make the Community Beautiful

Good citizens care about how their community looks. They don't litter. They take care of their homes. They also take care of places that everyone shares.

Children can help, too. They can recycle cans, bottles, and paper. They can plant trees and flowers for everyone to enjoy.

Wrap-Up

Good citizens work to make their community a better place. They get along with others. They look for ways to help. They work to make their community more beautiful.

CHAPTER 14

What Do Communities Share?

Our country is made up of many different communities.

In this chapter, you will learn about some of the things communities share to help each other.

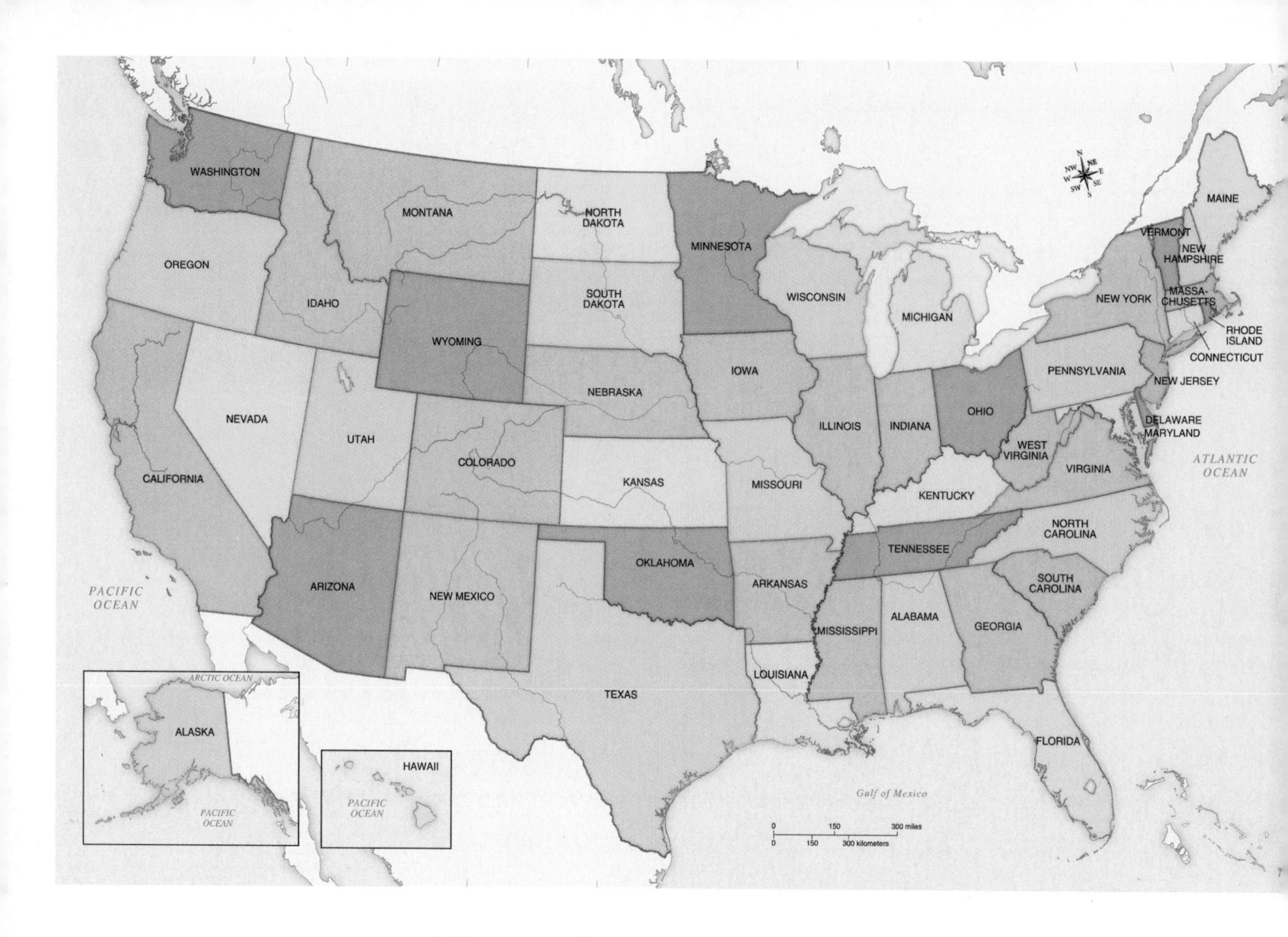

There Are Many Communities in Our Country

Some communities are big, and some are small. Some are rural. Some are urban. And some are suburban.

Every community is in a state. Our country has 50 states. Some states have deserts. Some are near the ocean. They are all part of our country, called the United States of America.

No community in our country has everything it needs. Communities share what they have.

Communities Share the Food They Grow

Food comes from many different places in our country. Fish comes from communities by the ocean. Beef comes from communities with lots of grass for cows to eat. Wheat and corn are grown by communities on the plains.

People move food from where it is produced to where it is needed.

Where do you think your favorite food comes from?

Communities Share the Goods They Make

Many of the things in your home were made in other communities in the United States.

Maybe your family car was made in Michigan. Maybe your classroom computer was made in California.

No community can make everything it needs and wants. We get many goods from other communities. They may get goods from our community.

Communities Share Their Special Places

Every community has special places. Some communities have beautiful beaches. Some have interesting cities.

People who travel to see other communities are called tourists. They go to see interesting places. They also go to meet people living in other communities.

Which communities in our country have you visited?

Communities Share Happy and Sad Times

People in communities like to share their happy times with others. They have festivals, celebrations, and games. They invite people from far away to enjoy these events with them.

Communities have sad times, too. Sometimes they must turn to other communities for help. A flood, tornado, or earthquake sometimes strikes a community. People all over the country send food, clothing, and money to help those in need.

Wrap-Up

Our country has many communities. Communities work together and share what they need and want. Some share the food they grow. Some share the things they make. Some share their special places. They also share their happy times and help each other in sad times.

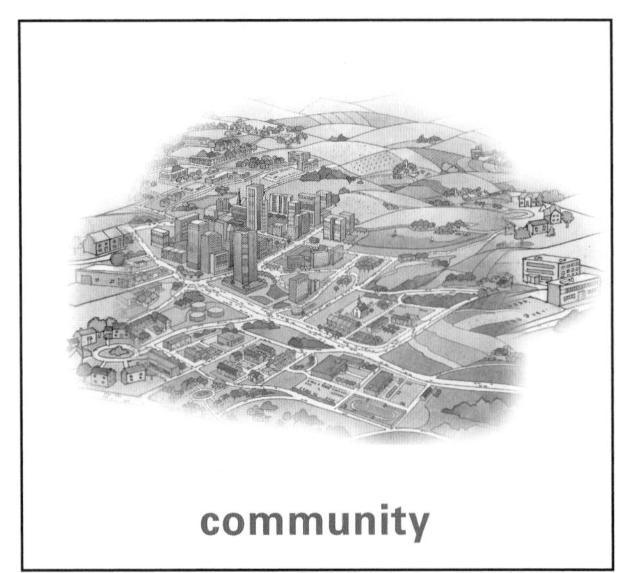

community

urban

rural

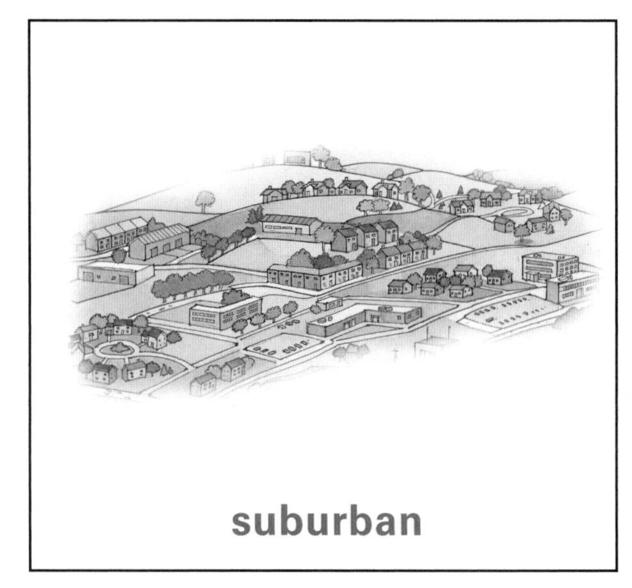

suburban

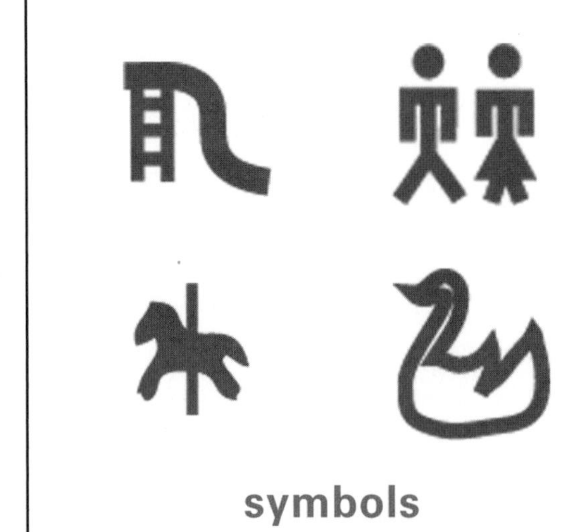

symbols

map key

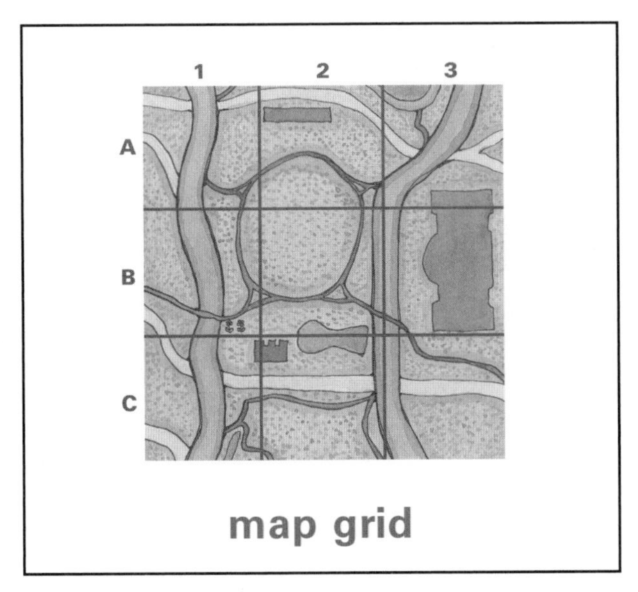

map grid

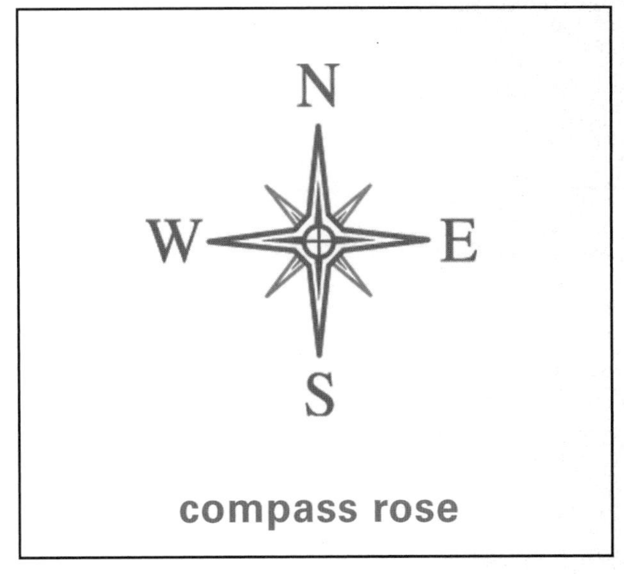

compass rose

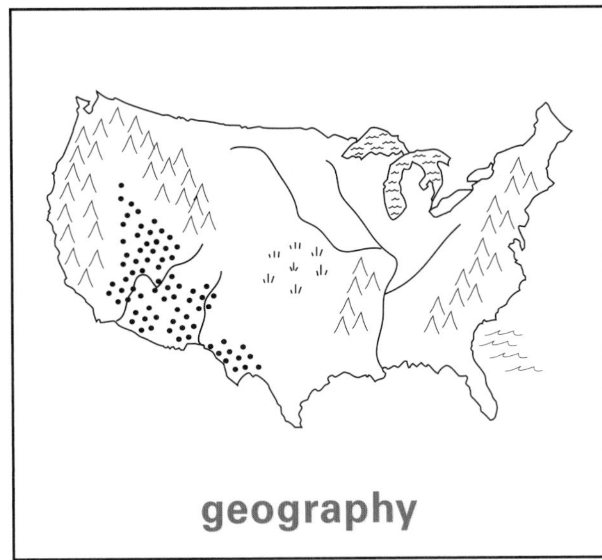
geography

mountains

valley

desert

plain

river

lake

island

ocean

environment

pollution

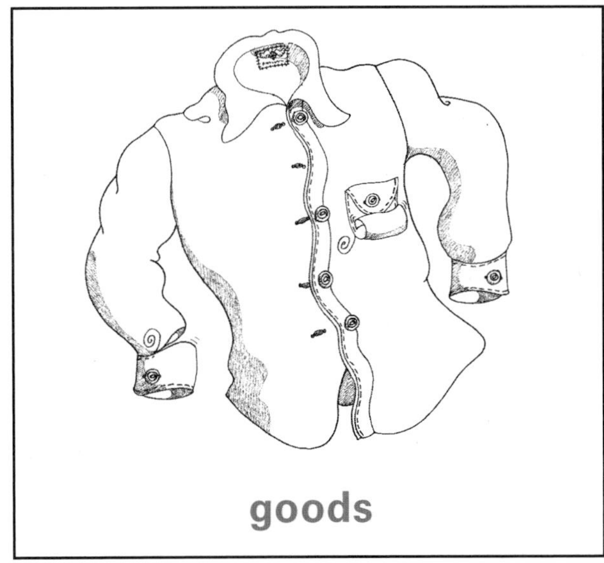

goods

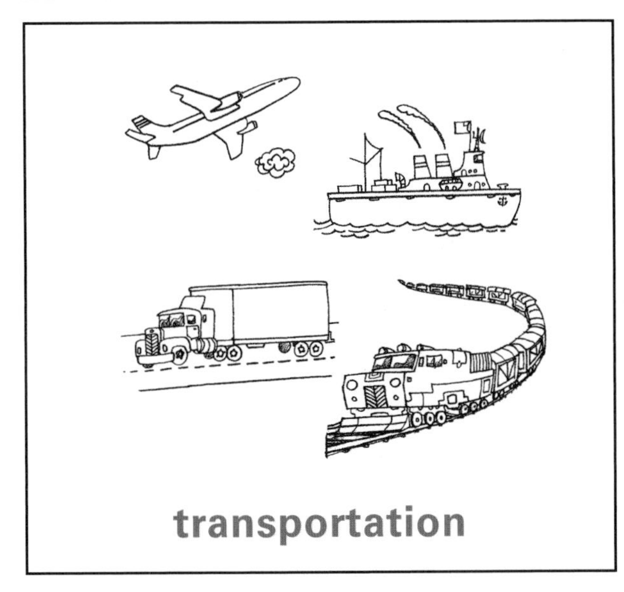

transportation

service job

need

want

history

earthquake

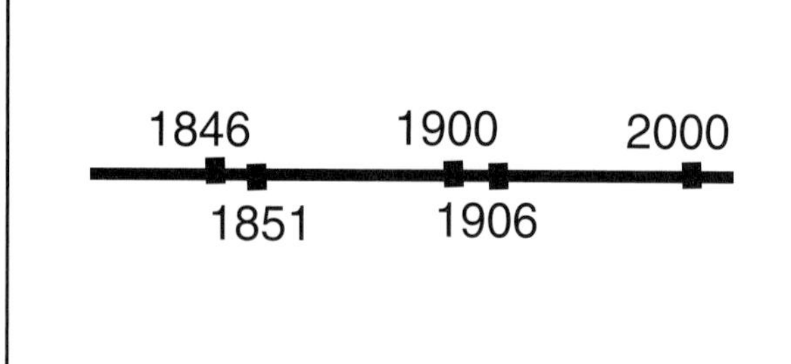

timeline

leaders

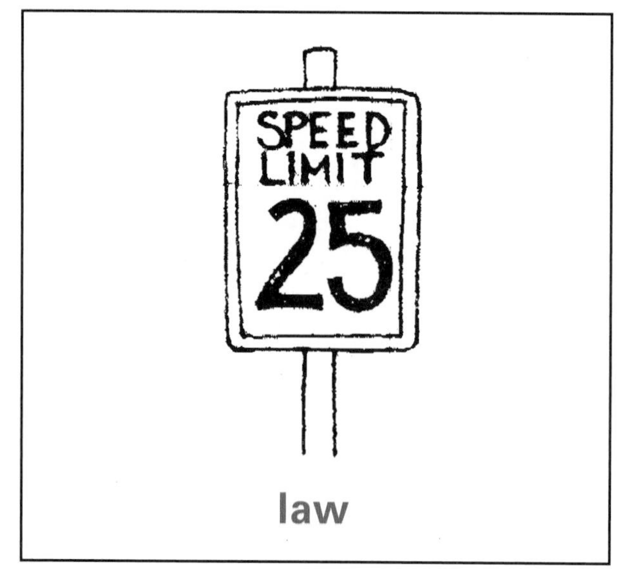

law

citizen

Credits

Contents

Chapter 1, Renata Lohman; **Chapter 2,** Len Ebert; **Chapter 3,** Renata Lohman; **Chapter 4,** Rosalind Solomon; **Chapter 5,** DJ Simison; **Chapter 6,** Doug Roy; **Chapter 7,** Len Ebert; **Chapter 8,** Jane McCreary; **Chapter 9,** Doug Roy; **Chapter 10,** Rosalind Solomon; **Chapter 11,** Len Ebert; **Chapter 12,** Carol Newsome; **Chapter 13,** Susan Jaekel; **Chapter 14,** Doug Roy

Chapter 1

2-3, Renata Lohman; **5,** © 2002 Walter Hodges/Getty Images/Stone; **6,** © 2002 Frank Whitney/Getty Images/The Image Bank; **7,** Corbis

Chapter 2

8-9, Len Ebert; **10,** Corbis; **11,** Corbis; **12,** Corbis; **14, lower,** Corbis

Chapter 3

16-17, Renata Lohman; **18, left,** Corbis; **19, lower left,** Corbis; **20,** Renata Lohman; **21,** Renata Lohman

Chapter 4

22-23, Rosiland Solomon; **24, upper,** Corbis; **24, lower,** © 2002 Angelo Cavalli/Getty Images/The Image Bank; **25, lower,** Corbis; **26, lower,** Corbis; **27, lower,** © 2002 Frans Lemmens/Getty Images/The Image Bank; **28,** Susan Jaekel

Chapter 5

30-31, DJ Simison; **32,** Corbis; **35, upper,** © 2002 Barbara Peacock/Getty Images/FPG; **36, lower,** © 2002 Charles Benes/Getty Images/FPG; **37,** © 2002 David Woodfall /Getty Images/Stone; **39,** Corbis

Chapter 6

40-41, Doug Roy; **43,** © 2002 Gabriel M. Covian/Getty Images/The Image Bank; **44,** Corbis; **45,** © 2002 David Frazier/Getty Images/Stone; **46,** © 2002 Mahaux Photography/Getty Images/The Image Bank; **47,** Corbis

Chapter 7

48-49, Len Ebert; **51, lower,** © 2002 Andy Sacks/Getty Images/Stone; **52, lower,** Corbis; **53,** Corbis

Chapter 8

54-55, Jane McCreary; **56,** Corbis; **59, upper,** © 2002 John Slater/Getty Images/FPG

Chapter 9

60-61, Doug Roy; **62,** © 2002 Yellow Dog Productions/Getty Images/The Image Bank; **63,** Corbis; **64,** ; **65,** Corbis

Chapter 10

66-67, Rosiland Solomon; **68,** Corbis; **69,** Corbis; **70,** San Francisco History Center, San Francisco Public Library; **71,** San Francisco History Center, San Francisco Public Library; **72, left,** Corbis; **72, right,** Corbis; **73, left,** Corbis; **73, right,** San Francisco History Center, San Francisco Public Library

Chapter 11

74-75, Len Ebert; **76,** University Archives, The University Library, The University of Illinois at Chicago; **77,** The Western Reserve Historical Society Library, Cleveland, Ohio; **78,** Archives and Special Collections on Women in Medicine, MCP Hahnemann University; **79,** courtesy of El Teatro Campesino, San Juan Bautista, California

Chapter 12

80-81, Carol Newsome; **82,** Corbis; **84, upper,** Corbis; **84, lower,** © 2002 Patti McConville/Getty Images/The Image Bank

Chapter 13

86-87, Susan Jaekel; **88,** courtesy of Christy Uyeno; **89,** © 2002 Terry Vine/Getty Images/Stone

Credits

Chapter 14

92-93, Doug Roy; **95, upper,** © 2002 Mark Segal/Getty Images/Stone; **95, lower,** © 2002 David W. Hamilton/Getty Images/The Image Bank; **97,** Corbis; **99,** Renata Lohman

Glossary

103, upper left, © 2002 David Woodfall/ Getty Images/Stone; **104, upper left,** Corbis; **104, upper right,** Corbis